Anthi Rose
Learns to
Skateboard

Deb Manikas
Illustrated by Robin Boyer

Outskirts Press, Inc.
http://www.outskirtspress.com

Paperback ISBN: 978-1-9772-4749-0
Hardback ISBN: 978-1-9772-4833-6

Illustrations by Robin Boyer © 2022 Debra Manikas Male. All rights reserved - used with permission.

Outskirts Press and the "OP" logo are trademarks belonging to Outskirts Press, Inc.

PRINTED IN THE UNITED STATES OF AMERICA

To my grandchildren with love:
Ryan, Emily, Devin, Cooper, Morgan,
Theo, Corinne, Benjamin, Nola
-DM

For Jess and Will—
Always find a way to do what you love.
-RB

 Find the hidden letters on pages 8-23 to see how Anthi Rose can learn to skateboard.

Anthi Rose

Learns to Skateboard

By Deb Manikas • Illustrated by Robin Boyer

Anthi Rose looked out the window at the night stars, choosing the brightest one to wish upon.

"Please, please, please make my important wish come true! I want a fast, cool skateboard like all the other kids. I want to be out there skateboarding with them every day."

Each night the week before her birthday,
Anthi Rose made her wish upon that star.

FINALLY her birthday arrived and her wish came true! Her Grandmama gave her a beautiful blue, yellow and green skateboard. It had silver, shiny wheels that purred when they spun. This skateboard was FAST, Anthi Rose could tell.

She couldn't wait to get on it and whizz around her neighborhood sidewalk with the other kids!

Right after breakfast, Anthi Rose put on her helmet,
grabbed her new skateboard and ran outside.
 "Hey guys," she yelled. "Look at my NEW
skateboard!"

All the kids gathered around.

"Try it out, Anthi!" the kids yelled.
"Race you to the corner!"

Anthi Rose's first try did not go very well.
She only went a few feet before she lost her
balance and hopped off.

"Gee," she said,
"This IS harder than it looks!"

Anthi Rose tried again. This time she stayed on longer, but the skateboard flipped out from under her feet. She had to jump off so she wouldn't get hurt. All the other kids whizzed past her on their fast skateboards.

Anthi Rose's third try ended when she fell off,
arms outstretched, skinning her elbow.
"Ouch!" she cried.

She picked up her skateboard and went
home. She got a bandaid for her scrape,
but her pride was hurt more.
Grandmama asked, "Are you going outside
to try your skateboard again?"

"No!" exclaimed Anthi Rose. "It is TOO HARD for me. I am scared. I thought I would be good at skateboarding, but I am not. I can't do it. I keep falling off."
She put her skateboard and helmet in the closet.

Each day, Anthi Rose would walk toward the closet,
She would quickly turn away.
"No," she thought, "Not today. I am still scared."
The skateboard and helmet collected dust in the
closet.

Anthi looked glumly out the window each day and watched the other kids whizzing past on their skateboards, waving to her from the sidewalk.

One day, Grandmama showed Anthi Rose a mouse hole in the garage. She said, "Anthi Rose, see that tiny mouse that lives in there?" Anthi Rose peered in the hole. The little brown field mouse scurried backward into the dark space.

Anthi Rose exclaimed, "It's afraid of me!
Why is it afraid of ME? I won't hurt it!"
Grandmama simply smiled.

The next day, Grandmama took Anthi Rose to check on the mouse again. Anthi Rose peeked in the hole. The little brown mouse scurried further back into the dark hole.

"Grandmama, the mouse needs to find food!
I brought it bread crumbs to eat and it still won't
come out! The mouse has to TRY to get food!
Even if it's scared."
Grandmama just smiled and said, "Exactly!"

The third day, Anthi Rose said, "Grandmama, let's go check on the mouse!" Grandmama and Anthi Rose peered into the hole. The little brown mouse was there, nibbling happily on a crust of bread. Anthi Rose said, "Look, Grandmama! It must have come out to get food. It's not afraid anymore!"

Grandmama asked, "How do you know that it is not afraid anymore?" Anthi Rose said, "Well, it was hungry! It HAD to leave its home!"
Grandmama said, "Exactly! The mouse was afraid, but came out anyway."

Anthi Rose smiled. She got up and ran into the house. Grandmama called after her, "Where are you going, Anthi Rose?"

"I am going skateboarding, of course! I may be afraid, but I CAN do this!" Anthi Rose happily put on her helmet and ran outside with her skateboard.

The End

Anthi's answer: PRACTICE

CPSIA information can be obtained
at www.ICGtesting.com
Printed in the USA
BVHW022126081121
621087BV00018B/34